Published by i-movo Limited

First Edition

First Printing of 1,000 copies only

i-movo Limited
Studio 518 The Metal Box Factory
30 Great Guildford Street
London SE1 0HS

Company Registration Number 7096894

i-movo.com

ISBN 978-1-5272-0347-1

Printed in England

KERSTIN FÄRNERT
NORDIC LIGHT

Skagen
Denmark

Introductory essay by Christopher de Hamel

the   son

Lovely

in blue

golden cloud

~~loud~~ behind

the sky ~~loud~~

so

and

Painted Fishing woman fr

in

the

It's half past nine on a Saturday evening and I'm with Kerstin Färnert in a restaurant on the quayside in Skagen, the most northern town in continental Europe. Only Grenen, the narrow spit of land honed to a point by the battering of the North and Baltic Seas lies between here and Norway.

We are looking at her paintings while she is sharing details about them, many are intensely personal. None have titles and the dates of most are unknown. According to the artist, these details are irrelevant because although the paintings are representational, they are subject to individual interpretation.

Ten years earlier, I had read Jonathan Coe's coming-of-age novel, *The Rotter's Club* and its sequel *The Closed Circle*. Both books feature Skagen at pivotal stages in the narrative, simply but vividly described. I wanted to see it for myself and, like the characters in the book, I wanted to dine at Pakhuset - preferably seated upstairs - surrounded by the "captains' wheels, rudders, chronometers and nautical decorations of every description".

It was here I came across an extraordinary series of paintings depicting the wild beauty of the coast and sea around Skagen, bathed in a luminous light. The artist was Kerstin Färnert. I'd never wanted to own a painting but I did now.

On my return home I contacted Kerstin. The terms of sale for her paintings were vague to say the least. Kerstin was also adamant that the sense of movement and intensity in her work would be lost on a website. If I was serious about acquiring one of her paintings, we would need to meet, in Skagen, to view them and discuss the matter.

It was not until May 2016, six years after my first visit, that I could visit Skagen again. I went to the restaurant early with my daughter so I could go and look at the paintings again to check they still had the same emotional resonance. They did.

After dinner, Kerstin invited us back to her home to look at more of her paintings. She showed me one she thought I might like. It struck a chord and we discussed its potential sale. After a few minutes, Kerstin shook her head sorrowfully and announced she could not bear to part with it. She felt her work had become too fragmented and only if her paintings were somehow curated in a single location could she bear to sell any more of them.

Although disappointed, I genuinely understood her position. Instead, applying the theory that talent and experience only serve as barriers to achievement, I offered to see how I could help. This book is the result.

Kerstin Färnert has a singular vision and a unique talent. Consequently, i-movo is delighted to help bring her work to a wider audience so that it might attain the recognition we feel it deserves.

David Tymm

after noork

Up in the Shy

warm feelings
              + clou
        for the h r

Glints   the lign 1

sea

At the northern tip of continental Europe, where the top of Denmark narrows eventually into a sand spit which divides the North Sea from the Kattegat, is a landscape and an environment which has obsessed artists and writers since the middle of the nineteenth century. Here are vast damp skies and seemingly endless bare dunes, forever shifting with the winds. The oceans are cold and dangerous. For two months in the high summer the days are long and the nights are hardly dark and the town of Skagen becomes a fashionable holiday destination. Its little harbour is filled with pleasure boats and the roads roar with camper-vans and luxury cars hurtling relentlessly up from Germany and Italy, especially, drawn by the fascination of pursuing the north road to its very end.

At Grenen, beyond the last lighthouse, cheering visitors stand with a foot in each ocean and then bustle back into Skagen to the restaurants and bars. By September, however, the nights start drawing in and the summerhouses are boarded up again. Skagen reverts to what it has always been, a working fishing town, a vast modern industry set in a very ancient land - and seascape. In the winter it is very cold and the days are short. The old fishermen's and merchants' cottages are built well back from the sea and its relentless wind. The extreme edges of the red tiled roofs, in lines up the gables, are painted white, like winter snow driven into the eaves. There is money to be made from the oceans but it has never been easy.

This essay concerns a group of extraordinary paintings by a single artist, mostly executed here in Skagen. Since 1994 there has been a continual exhibition of many of these pictures around the walls of a restaurant and bar called Pakhuset, a converted fish factory on the waterfront of Skagen harbour. Holiday-makers pushing and jostling for tables probably hardly notice the paintings. There are no labels or explanations and there are certainly no prices. The artist's name is not obviously apparent. If the pictures are for sale at all (which is not entirely clear, even to the artist), these are no pretty seaside souvenirs. There are no yachts or sandcastles or picturesque views of the town. There are no children visible in these scenes.

Come instead to Pakhuset in February. Dash from the car park, hunched against the blizzard, and pull open the door. Close it behind you, shutting out the sound of the rain, the groan of fog-horns and the noise of the fishing industry on the fore-shore. Shake your sou'wester and call for a Danish beer. Then look at the paintings: vast stormy landscapes, biting winds, shapes which in the half-light reveal themselves to be seamen with their nets and women in the fish factory, wet, cold and muggy. They are pictures which evoke all five senses; you can hear the weather, smell the fish and taste the dried salt. There are smudges of grey, restless blue and dashes of brilliant colour. They are hypnotic and puzzling.

You gaze at a painting and it seems to change shape, as if you had wiped the condensation from the window and it has frosted over again even as you do so. You cannot quite make out what these people in their private world are actually doing, or even sometimes whether they are people at all. Ask the artist and she will fix you with her genial aquamarine blue eyes and shrug mildly: "You tell me", she will say.

Kerstin Färnert was born at Göteborg in Sweden in 1943. She studied at the École des Beaux Arts in Wavre in Belgium in the mid-1970s. Her pictures were first shown in public in the town hall in Wavre in 1976. Her early work is graceful and pretty, often infused with the colouring of Matisse. Some reflect Mediterranean family holidays, light and rapidly-sketched images floating on their canvases. They show a facility with colour, dexterity and joy, with none of the brooding quality of the later pictures.

Färnert returned to Sweden and studied further at the Konstskolan in Stockholm in 1982-84. In May 1984 her pictures won the first and third prizes in the final exhibition of the work of all students in her year. She was awarded a visit to Sicily. Her pictures appeared in exhibitions in Stockholm and elsewhere, including Paris in 1987. In November (in the winter) 1987, Färnert came first to Skagen. She eventually settled in a nineteenth-century fisherman's cottage in Østerbyvei.

The town is probably the most famous in Scandinavia for its colony of painters at the turn of the nineteenth and twentieth centuries, gathered around P. S. Krøyer (1851-1909), Michael and Anna Ancher (1849-1927 and 1859-1935) and others, with many stylistic descendants. Note this point, but then compare the work of the so-called Skagen painters and that of Färnert. It is very different indeed.

The Skagen school is one of narrative. Their pictures (and there are many in the Skagen Museum, still within a few yards of where they were painted) are scenes from the unfolding cycle of life: christenings, childhood, birthdays, pastimes, walking on the beach, bringing in the nets, old age and death. These are images set in a context, with events which must have lead up to what is shown and with consequences expected. Every picture illustrates a story, which the viewer guesses from a single moment in the tale. There may even be a moral. The fisherman has drowned; we see him brought in; the new widow re-begins her life. There is always an implicit narrative, even in the weather-battered faces of the townsmen painted originally around the panelling of Brøndrum's hotel.

Kerstin Färnert's paintings are concerned with feelings or senses but not with storytelling. There is nothing beforehand or afterwards. There is colour and movement and sensation. They represent and recreate the moments when the heart leaps or cries out but there is no essential moral, except perhaps to share the experience of being human.

The paintings belong, in fact, to a much larger tradition than the more illustrative painters of Skagen. This is what is loosely called the northern romantic movement. It goes back to the eighteenth century, to the beginnings of philosophical romanticism. Curiously, Edmund Burke's essay, *Philosophical Enquiry into the Origins of our Ideas of the Sublime and the Beautiful,* 1756, sets the scene more closely than the photographic compilations of the Anchers and Krøyer.

The romantics rejoiced in the wildness of nature, which has no story: it just exists. Human participation, if there is any, is one of losing a struggle against the elements or fate. The painting by Caspar David Friedrich of the *Monk by the Sea* bewildered spectators when it was first shown in Berlin in 1810, for it is seemingly empty. JMW Turner's late paintings share a great deal with Färnert's landscapes - evocations of steam, storm, haze and sunset, swirling blizzards and tempestuous seas. Emile Nolde too stands firmly within northern romanticism, with his low and hazy horizons and melancholic unpopulated landscapes along the coast of Schleswig-Holstein.

From these we move quite easily into the winter nightmares of Edvard Munch and the patterns of colour in the Danish painter Oluf Høst. These are people who have experienced their environment. Høst himself, who was born and worked on the remote Baltic island of Bornholm, kept notebooks which he called his *Synteser of set, læst og oplevet*, 'Syntheses of sight, reading and experience', thoughts, feelings, ideas and impressions, both of nature and of people, which he expressed in paint.

In Färnert's paintings we certainly see syntheses of her experience: in the fragmentation and blackness of her art when her first marriage fell apart and she migrated to Denmark; in the struggle of her first years in Skagen, working in the fish factory to earn enough to live, cold, bleak and touchingly human pictures, damp and cold in the early mornings; in the joy and gaiety of her new-found love; in the gloom of her fiancé's unexpected death, and the gradual resurrection through melancholy into peace and a circle of friends.

The romantic poets, like Goethe and Wordsworth, always struggled with the dilemma of being a product of nature and yet not quite a part of it. There may be something of this too in Färnert's own life: Swedish but living in Denmark, sharing a Scandinavian ancestry with her neighbours but always an outsider, a well-known member of a close community but forever on the edge, like Friedrich's monk. A poem she herself wrote for her fiancé in 1991 about the beauty of solitude concludes:

Du själ
Du tärs av sorg
Du njuter lycka
Lycka
Du stora hav
Din styrka
Din skönhet
Din gåtfullhet
Mitt hav.

You soul
You are consumed by sorrow
You delight in joy
Joy
You great ocean
Your strength
Your beauty
Your mystery
My ocean.

Reference to the artist's soul implies spirituality. There is undoubtedly a sacredness in northern romantic painting but it is not at all the conventional Christianity of the Mediterranean south. It is a response to far older and more primitive Nordic beliefs in thunder, sea and earth. Where the Anchers and Krøyer show dutiful Lutherans clustered around their printed Bibles or walking to church, the Scandinavian romantic painters touch the human soul at an infinitely more ancient and elemental level, in responding to light and darkness, fire, water and earth. There is no time for the cosy Skagen interiors and urbane and homely Sunday dining rooms. These are paintings which convey a human religious experience which is tens of thousands of years old.

Kerstin Färnert lives alone in a tiny nineteenth-century cottage, once owned by the fisherman Peder Nielsen Normand (1828-1875) and his daughter. The garden beyond spills out from the french windows. It is dominated by a grassy mound once surmounted by a flagpole, leading down to a distant wall from which one can glimpse the sea, her ocean (as the poem calls it). In the summer the garden is a medley of colours and patterns, both in what is grown and in objects artlessly placed on a long wooden garden table. A one-eared cat called Julia wanders happily among the geraniums. The outside walls of the house are typically Skagen yellow. The doors and windows are sky blue, or the blue of Scandinavian eyes. Upstairs, up a staircase almost as steep as a ship's ladder, is her studio.

Paintings from all periods of her life clutter the room. Her business cards as an artist used to give her name beside the words 'Harbour, Sea, Dune', which form the title of this essay,

but it is not as simple as that. Watch how Färnert paints. She will prop up a canvas and rapidly cover it with colour, light and dark, warm and cold, ever changing the shapes and compositions, with (at least at the beginning) no decided subject. She may completely repaint the canvas very many times, often turning it round to reconsider the balance of colour and pattern and beginning again the other way up. This stage can take weeks, and she comes away emotionally drained and physically exhausted as gradually a pleasing pattern of colours begins to emerge.

One result of this endless re-working is that every finished picture consists of many layers of different-colours, dried and covered over, as smooth and hard as enamel but as textured as wind-driven landscape itself, or an ill-tended garden where one kind of flower dies and another grows in its place, imperceptibly changing the whole effect from day to day. The colours mixed on her palette may sometimes lend themselves to a particular theme, like the sandy-coloured tussock of the Skagen dunes or the pinky grey of a winter sky, but she is not bothered by any deliberate reality at this stage. There are no straight lines.

There is no direct copying from the outside world. Färnert will paint over and over again and then stand back and, with almost childlike astonishment, she will finally observe with a giggle or a gasp of delight that the canvas seems to be evolving into a recognisable or pleasing design. She will add a few careful strokes, and the subconscious design becomes, at least on the surface, one of her fairly small repertoire of familiar compositions of an old man hunched over his nets, or women scaling fish into wooden vats, or a face or a storm at sea. She stops just before the picture becomes completely representational. The composition is still fluid and alive. The trick is knowing when the painting is ready.

It is this element of chance which makes the paintings so fascinating. When one of Turner's paintings was exhibited at the Royal Academy in 1846, both he and the public were astonished to realise that the random impasto of a golden sky seemed to have focused itself into the shape of an angel. Färnert's finished paintings are assigned a primary subject but nothing gives her more delight than noticing other unintentional images concealed in the brushstrokes or if buyers of the pictures find them later: swirls that in a certain light look like a bird, for example, or the face of her husband whom, unaware, she was perhaps thinking of while painting. She might say that what she has seen or read or experienced had somehow become a pattern that seemed appropriate, without really knowing why; and that ability to recognise the moment when a painting's purpose is fulfilled is the finest way to express human emotion. It also means that a seemingly empty picture suddenly acquires human life when the viewer himself participates in the scene by reinterpreting what is painted. It is not just a vacant landscape but a landscape in which you yourself are the human figure. It would be rather like standing in a winter's storm or a crowded street and suddenly sensing a moment of beauty, danger, fear, happiness or other emotion.

The setting would be the result of chance; but the feelings it evoked, if the moment could be recognised and preserved, would be universal. Colours are crucial in Färnert's pictures but it is not merely harmony or prettiness. Someone once told the American painter Mark Rothko that they enjoyed his use of colour. He replied: "I am not interested in colour or form or anything else ... I am interested only in expressing the basic human emotions - tragedy, ecstasy, doom, and so on - and the fact that lots of people break down and cry when confronted with my pictures shows that I communicate with those basic human emotions. The people who weep before my pictures are having the same religious experience I had when I painted them. And if you, as you say, are moved only by their colour relationships, you have missed the point."

Kerstin Färnert is a very different painter from the artists of the Skagen style, but the reality of Skagen is echoed in all her pictures: the vast lonely emptiness, the beauty and the power of the long northern nights and the treacherous seas, and the everlasting patience and monotony of the fishing business. It is not the staged chocolate-box world of the summer visitors to Skagen but is the universality of human experience, and that, in short, is what makes her paintings so hypnotically fascinating.

Christopher de Hamel
Fellow, Corpus Christi College
Cambridge

8

Flower theme

1984
Oil on canvas

10

The happy bowl

1990
Oil on canvas

12

The red chair

1998
Oil on canvas

14

Flower

Date unknown
Oil on canvas

Stockholm in the morning hour

1982
Oil on canvas

18

Sicily

1984
Oil on canvas

20

Painted before I came to Skagen

1985
Oil on canvas

22

The dancing glasses

1992
Oil on canvas

24

Small and back from the big sea

1997
Oil on canvas

Two girls with the blue wall

1992
Oil on canvas

Friends

1999
Oil on canvas

Me and Tores mysterious face

1995
Oil on canvas

Light atmosphere at the fish factory

1994
Oil on canvas

34

Mind

1996
Oil on canvas

Beauty

1998
Oil on canvas

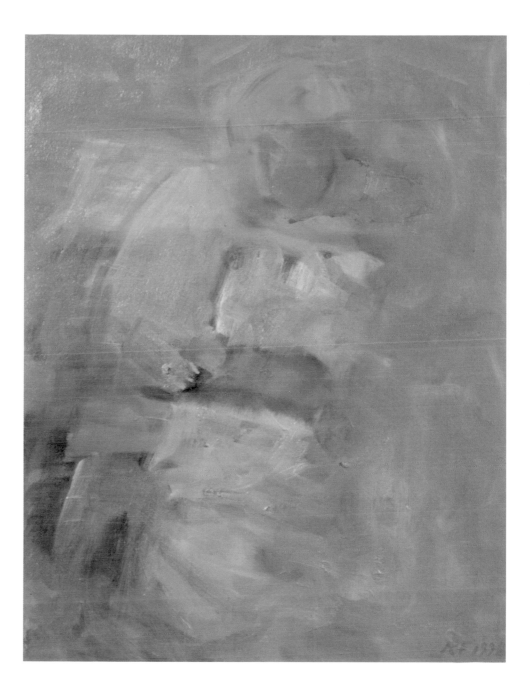

38

Yellow girl

1999
Oil on canvas

Hard work

1996
Oil on canvas

Fish factory

1995
Oil on canvas

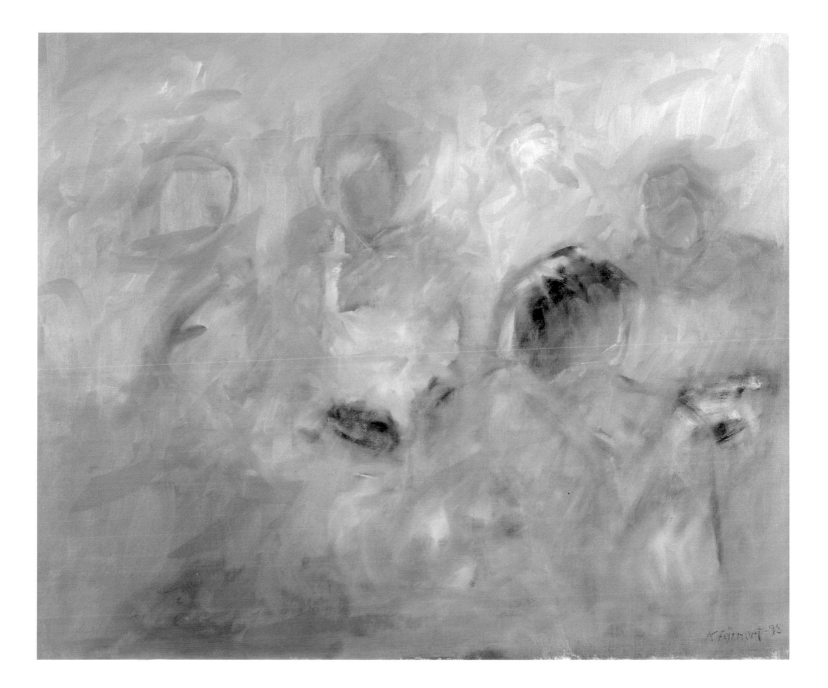

44

Together

1996
Oil on canvas

46

Good ambience

1996
Oil on canvas

48

Fish factory with portrait

Fish factory with portrait

2006
Oil on canvas

50

1999
Oil on canvas

52

1996
Oil on canvas

54

Splicing in harbour

56

Vagn Madsen, my good neighbour

1999
Oil on canvas

58

In the harbour

1993
Oil on canvas

60

Struggling

1993
Oil on canvas

62

Salmon

1993
Oil on canvas

64

The dog and her companion

1993
Oil on canvas

66

Jacket and window in blue

1993
Oil on canvas

68

1992
Oil on canvas

70

Warm evening

1993
Oil on canvas

Warm feelings

1993
Oil on canvas

74

Up in the sky

1993
Oil on canvas

76

Gone with the wind

1993
Oil on canvas

Midsummer fire on the beach of Sønder Strand

1993
Oil on canvas

80

Beloved land

1993
Oil on canvas

82

Lovely grey-toned dune

1994
Oil on canvas

84

Golden cloud

1997
Oil on canvas

86

Greytone

1998
Oil on canvas

Transparency on the edge

1997
Oil on canvas

Dunes

1990
Oil on canvas

92

Dunes

1990
Oil on canvas

94

Storm on the shore

1998
Oil on canvas

98

My light and darkness

2002
Oil on canvas

100

Heaven & earth

2000
Oil on canvas

Longing for the horizon

2006
Oil on canvas

104

Endless

1992
Oil on canvas

106

Missing inferno

2004
Oil on canvas

Kerstin Färnert was born in Gotheburg, Sweden, in 1943. She lived with her family until moving to London and then Brussels in 1971, where she studied at the École des Beaux Arts in Wavre, Belgium. Returning to Sweden in 1981, Färnert studied at the Konstskolan (School of Art). Competing with 140 other entries, she won the first prize in the final exhibition for her Flower Theme in Oil, presented to her by noted industrial designer Count Sigvard Bernadotte (born, Prince Sigvard of Sweden) and his wife, Marianne.

The prize provided the means to travel and work in Europe including the opportunity to capture the mediterranean light at the site of Naxos, an ancient city perched on a rocky headland on the eastern coast of Sicily. The work produced here subsequently formed the basis of her 1984 exhibition on the island.

By the time Färnert exhibited in Paris in 1987 with the itinerant Gothenburg gallery of Victor Rydberg, she had already established a reputation in Sweden. In Paris, together with nine other emerging artists, she exhibited in the Galerie Jean Camion on the Rue des Beaux Arts, the Parisian street that is home to some of the most prestigious galleries in the city. According to critic Chris Fornse, writing in Swedish Daily newspaper, Svenska Dagbladet "The artist who created the greatest enthusiasm amongst the discriminating art connoisseurs is Kerstin Färnert whose tender landscapes in oil correspond with the french perception of 'nordic light'".

Färnert had first visited Skagen in November 1987, returning to live there in 1990. Circumstances dictated she needed to take a job and did so, gutting herring in a fish factory, one of the many experiences of living in Skagen that has informed her work.

Färnert first exhibited her paintings in Skagen at the Clausens Hotel in 1988, a year after her first visit, and then again in 1992 at the historic White Lighthouse, an octagonal tower just north of the town made redundant in 1858 by the newer, taller lighthouse two kilometres up the coast at Grenen. Throughout the 1990s Färnert regularly exhibited at Restaurant Pakhuset ('packing house') where her paintings still hang.

Early works include water-colours but recent paintings are all in oil, often using a palette knife lending a unique texture to the work. Reviewing an exhibition at Staffen Thelin's gallery in Hassela, Äke Hanaeus, art critic of a Swedish newspaper Sundvalls Tidning noted that, "She wants to produce a type of picture where detail is not important. Instead, she wants to present a syntheses of experience in nature, often where the sky and water are the main contents," and that, "the different tones in colour merge in a way that one gets a musical sensation of the paintings."

Kerstin Färnert still lives in Skagen in a nineteenth-century fisherman's cottage in Østerbyvei, surrounded by the dunes, sea and sky that were the inspiration for so many of her paintings.

Kerstin Färnert, prisad i Paris och väl värd uppmärksamhet i Hassela. "Karisma" och "Hela havet stormar" är de tavlor hon är omgiven av.

Bilder med palettkniv

Staffan Thelin i Ölsjön, Hassela, brukar varje sommar kombinera sin egen utställning i ateljén, där han visar sitt silver- och guldsmide, med någon form av bildkonst. Nu har han som gästutställare Kerstin Färnert från Stockholm.

Hon är född 1943 i Göteborg. Först studerade hon utomlands vid Académie des Beaux Arts i Wavre i Belgien, därefter vid Konstskolan i Stockholm.

Nu vsiar hon oljemåleri, mest utfört med palettkniv eftersom hon vill åstadkomma en typ av bilder där detaljerna inte är viktiga, hon vill i stället framställa synteser av naturupplevelser, gärna där hav och himmel är huvudinnehållet. Förr kallade somliga skribenter detta för symfoniskt expressionism.

Det betydde att de olika färgklangerna var så instämda i va-

Ett motiv med exotisk prägel av Kerstin Färnert.

rann att man kunde få en musikalisk upplevelse av målningarna. Sådana bilder behöver inte föreställa något. De är sig själva.

Staffan Thelin visar sin per-

sonligt formade smideskonst, mest silver ibland också med inslag av guld. Han är inte rädd för att ta djärva grepp.

ÅKE HANÆUS

GALLERI LINNÉ
Svartbacksgatan 22 — Uppsala 018/15.28.00

KERSTIN FÄRNERT

Olja

Mitt hav

19/1 - 30/1

Vernissage lörd 19/1 1991
kl 12 - 16

Tisd-fred 11.30 - 17.30, lörd 10 - 15, sönd 12 - 15

Välkommen!

Parisgalleri med svenskar

Paris (G-P): Ungt svenskt måleri kan det var något för fransmän? Ja, det hoppas Göteborgsgalleriet Victor Rydberg som rest till Paris med nio "okända" svenska konstnärer i bagaget.

Under ett par veckor har man kunnat hyra lokaler på en av Paris bästa gallerigator, Rue des Beaux Arts, alldeles intill konstfack.

Vissa av utställarna som göteborgskan Kerstin Färnert, Inga Berndin-Svens-

son och silversmeden Staffan Thelin har redan skaffat sig gedigen utställningsvana och ett visst namn i Sverige. Men andra som Gun Gudjonson, Ulla-Britt Hill, Sara Berndtsson, Lena Wiroth, Emhå Mellby och Ingrid Fröslin är fortfarande ganska okända. Den som väckt mest uppståndelse hos den kräsna parisiska publiken är trots allt göteborgskan Kerstin Färnert vars skira landskap i olja stämmer med fransmännens uppfattning om det nordiska ljuset.

CHRIS FORSNE

| École des Beaux Arts | 1975 - 1976 | Wavre, Belgium |
| Kungliga Konsthögskolan | 1982 - 1984 | Stockholm, Sweden |

Stadhuset	1976	Wavre, Belgium
Konstskolans Höstutställning	1983	Stockholm, Sweden
Kulturhuset	1983	Stockholm, Sweden
De Refuserades Salong	1984	Stockholm, Sweden
Stipendium og uställning	1984	Maxos, Sicily
Saltsjöateljen	1986	Saltsjöbadén, Sweden
Galleri Jean Camion	1987	Paris, France
Galleri Staffan Thelin	1988	Hassela, Sweden
Clausens Hotel	1988	Skagen, Denmark
Saltsjöateljen	1990	Saltsjöbadén, Sweden
Galleri Linné	1991	Uppsala, Sweden
Blasius Knst & Antik AB	1991	Stockholm, Sweden
Handelsmässan	1992	Stockholm, Sweden
Det Hvide Fyr	1992	Skagen, Denmark
Sparekassen Nordjylland	1994	Skagen, Denmark
Galleri Killebacken	1994	Killebacken, Sweden
Niels Skiverens Gaard	1994	Tversted, Denmark
Restaurant Pakhuset	1994 - 2017	Skagen, Denmark
Vingården	1996	Odense, Denmark
Saltsjöateljen	1996	Saltsjöbadén, Sweden
Banegarden	1997	Aabenraa, Denmark

Skagens milda ljus

En utpräglad kolorist med utomordentlig förmåga att syntetisera sina synintryck av ett landskap till skönt och vilsamt måleri är säsongens första utställare hos Galleri Linné. Kerstin Färnerts Skagenmålningar är tröst för trötta ögon och sinnen, skriver Cristina Karlstam.

◇ DEN LYCKLIGA SKÅLEN — det låter som titeln på en målning av Evert Lundquist: en solgul skål mot blekblå grund, ingenting mer, det enklaste föremål utvalt som symbol för en livsattityd. Målning-

Galleri Linné: Kerstin Färnert, måleri.

en finns just nu hos Galleri Linné, som inleder vårens rad av utställningar med en liten finstämd och lysande vacker serie målningar av en 'sensibel kolorist (t o m 30 januari).

Kerstin Färnert är född i Göteborg, utbildad i Belgien och sedan en tid tillbaka bosatt i Skagen på Danmarks allra nordligaste udde där två hav möts. Skagen, dess översinnligt vita ljus, dess gula sanddyner och dess osannolikt blå himmel är också temat i hennes utställning. Skagen i morgondis och dagsljus. Skagen efter stormen med åskblått hav. Skagen nattetid då sandens gula ljus fortfar att tränga igenom natturörkret.

◇ ONEKLIGEN krävs det ett visst mått av konstnärligt mod att ge sig i kast med ett landskap som fått sin bildmässiga gestaltning av storheter som P S Kröyer, Anna Ancher, Michael Ancher. Skagenmålarna som, trodde man kanske, en gång för alla präglat vår bild av detta säregna landskap och dess märkliga dagrar. Kerstin Färnert gör heller inga försök att ta upp kampen med dessa bilder; hon väljer en annan väg, syntetiserar sina intryck av landskapet och dess färger och formulerar sig med uteslutande koloristiska medel. Därmed blir också hennes bilder något annat och mycket mer än minnen av ett landskap. Hela spektret av mänskliga känslor och stämningar får i hennes bilder sitt visuella uttryck.

Det här är bildkonst för trötta sinnen och oroliga ögon, motbilder att vila i när vardag och omvärld känns alltför tunga. Skagens milda ljus fångat med färg på duk!

CRISTINA KARLSTAM

KULTURNYTT

Nordiska rådets litteraturpris har för 1991 tilldelats den samiske författaren Nils Aslak Valkeapää. Han får priset för lyriksamlingen Solen, min far. I sin motivering skriver prisjuryn: "Författaren har skapat ett verk som knyter samman forntid och nutid, dokumen-

misk kulturhistoria och visar läsarna det samiska språkets rikedom. Ordens dubbla och flertydiga innehåll inspirerar läsaren till reflektion och ger det samiska folket en tro på det egna språkets bärkraft och ger en berättigad självmedvetenhet i ...

DIPLOM

Oh, starka sköna
ensomhet!

Arbete, kärlek som gjorts
synlig

Sköna kamp
Lång promenad
Leende klitter
tankar ...

I "mauve" ger
sydvästen hals

Vindpinad

Återvänder till ljuvliga
toner som skänkts mitt
slitna öra om och om
igen

- Hur kunde jag?
- Hur jag kunde?
Punctum maximum!

Du själ
Du tärs av sorg
Du njuter lycka

Lycka
Du stora hav
Din styrka
Din skönhet
Din gåtfullhet
Mitt hav.

Kerstin Färnert
Skagen 1991

Follow your dreams

If while pursuing distant dreams
Your bright hopes turn to gray,
Don't wait for reassuring words
Or hands to lead the way.

For seldom will You find a soul
With dreams the same as yours.
Not often will another help You
Pass through untried doors.

If inner forces urge you
To take a course unknown,
Be ready to go all the way,
Yes, all the way alone.

That's not to say You shouldn't
Draw lessons from the best;
Just don't depend on lauding words
To spur You on your quest.

Find confidence within your heart
And let it be your guide.
Strive ever harder toward your dreams
And they wont be denied.

Bruce B Wilmer

Artist's Acknowledgements

Gunnar Färnert for choosing the Flower theme in
the final exhibition at Konstskolan, Stockholm

Anna Färnert for sending me *Follow your dreams* by
Bruce B. Wilmer after I moved to Skagen in 1990

Erik Färnert for cutting wood in the garden
and saying "Ma, this is the closest to paradise"

Nils Färnert for his support
Loveliest Ellinor, Elsa, Ida, Hugo, Lova & Simone

My whole family and friends

Special warm thanks to Christoher & Mette de Hamel
for always encouraging me in my work

David & Charlotte Tymm for
their initiative to produce this book

Karen & Hans Sund at Pakhuset, Skagen, for good
'ambiance' and support for over 20 years

All my customers here in Skagen and abroad

Photographer Terje Gr. Løchen for his fine work

Photographer Peter Brüen for the
fine 'raw' photo in the fish factory

Set in Univers & Caslon

Photography of paintings by Terje Grønneberg Løken,
Trollstien, Drammen, Norway

Digitisation of large & medium format transparencies by
Max Communications, Chislehurst, Kent, UK
using Hasselblad X5 48-bit image scanner

Printed on Novatech silk by Quddos Printing Solutions,
Swanscombe, Kent, UK

Designed by Tilly Sleven

Biography by Charlotte Tymm

Thanks to Philip Abel, Sebastian Abugattas, Paul Brett,
Andrew & Leigh Cantwell, Gunnar Färnert,
Mette & Christopher de Hamel and the directors
and staff of i-movo for their support of this project

Edited by David Tymm